A GUIDE

TO CONFESSION

Fr Bede Rowe

A GUIDE
TO CONFESSION

veníte ad me omnes qui laborátis et oneráti estis
et ego refíciam vos

Published in 2011
by Lulu.com
www.lulu.com

ISBN 978-1-4467-8738-0

Dedicated
to
Fr Alexander Redman
and
Fr Anthony Meredith S.J.

Contents

1

INTRODUCTION

Many years ago an old Jesuit gave me a valuable piece of advice. He said to me that if I ever wanted to know how my spiritual life was going, all I needed to do was ask myself one simple question:

"When was the last time I went to Confession?"

When he gave me this advice, I looked a little puzzled. I had thought that I would have had to go in for some deep soul searching or go to visit a spiritual director. "No" he said, "just ask yourself that question."

Of course he was right. It is, I think, the gift of good old-fashioned Jesuits to be right about most things.

What he was saying was that Confession is a weather vane for the state of the soul. In the years that have passed I have found this Priest's words to be true. If it has been too long since I have been to Confession then there is something going wrong with my relationship with God, and often I am hiding, or rather stupidly trying to hide, something from Him. In my experience as a Priest I can honestly say that Confession is the first Sacrament to disappear on the way to lapsing from the faith.

There are many reasons for this. The main one is that lapsing from faith is running from God and running from yourself. Confession is the Sacrament of honesty: sometimes brutal honesty.

Let's face it, you have given up on the diet when you no longer step on the scales, and you've given up on faith when you no longer go to Confession. Like the diet, however, it's never too late! But you have to face up to what is going on, you have to put yourself at rights with God and receive His grace and His truth.

That way your spiritual life will flourish and my Jesuit will be proved right... again!

2

WHAT'S IN A NAME?

There is nowadays a little confusion as to what the Sacrament is called. It is one of those things which changed in the recent past. I always refer to it as 'Confession' mainly because that is what people usually call it. I think that there is a great value in using terms which have always been used. You know where you stand then. I used to have many conversations which went along the following lines:

"I will be available for Reconciliation after Mass."

"What's that?"

"Confession."

"Ohhh, Confession...."

So it is easier, to my simple mind, to call something by a name which everyone knows. The Sacrament is also known as "Reconciliation", "Penance", "Reconciliation and Penance", "Confession and Reconciliation" and if you randomly picked up bulletins from Churches you would see it described as all of these things. The Catechism of the Catholic Church (the hand book of what we believe) calls it all of these titles and more (§§ 1422-1424).

All of these titles reflect elements of the Sacrament. There has to be confession of sins, and there has to be penance experienced and imposed so that reconciliation can take place. They all take place one after the other. First there is confession of sins and then once that has happened a penance is imposed. Only after this can reconciliation take place and be spoken out loud.. All of these names show elements of the Sacrament, and as we go through the Sacrament we shall see that all of them are essential.

So really, you could use any or all of these terms. If we think that the name of the Sacrament should describe everything that occurs within it, then we'll be here all day, and run out of space every time we try to write it down! Most of the titles mention only one part of the Sacrament. I just think that it is easier to use a name which everyone is familiar with, both inside and outside the Church.

The name does not matter, but what it brings about does. The sinner is reconciled with God and can go on their way without the weight of the spiritual consequences of their actions upon their soul - the scar remains, but the weight is gone.

Call it what you like… just make sure that you come!

3

PREPARATION FOR COMMUNION

Of all the Church's seasons Lent is the one most associated with Confession. In fact in many parishes it is the only time that Confession is mentioned. Thankfully, there has been a revival of reminding people that it is a good thing to go to Confession during Advent, the other great season of preparation. But if Lent is the only time that it is pushed, then I'm not decrying that at all, because Confession at just one time of the year is much better than no Confession at all!

So why are Lent and Confession so closely associated? Well, Catholics, if they are able to, are still under the obligation to receive Holy Communion once a year "at Easter or there abouts". To receive Communion, one must be in a state of grace and states of grace come about through the confession of sins. The things simply follow on from one another. Confession and Lent, therefore, are joined because Lent is a preparation for Easter and at Easter you receive Our Lord in Holy Communion.

It used to be the case that if you went into a Catholic Church on a Saturday morning you would see huge long line of people waiting to go to Confession. If we are honest, and there is no point not being, it has been a number of years since that was the case. It is not that people were greater sinners in the past than they are now. Next time you're at Holy Mass, look around you. Do you think that all those old people been up to worse things than you? No, of course not. But they had a much greater appreciation of the meaning if not of Confession, then of Holy Communion. They would not have thought for a moment of going to Holy Communion if there was anything at all on their conscience. It was (and is) better to go to Confession, just in case.

Not only does Confession absolve sin, but it also is the way of making sure that we are in a fit state to receive Communion. The two are intimately connected as they are both important elements of the spiritual life.

I suppose some may ask if any of this matters. Is God bothered if we have been up to a few things that we shouldn't have, and then still receive Communion? I think that is a pretty sad question, but let's look at it anyway.

I would ask you to consider two things:

Do you really think that you are the best person to decide if what you have done is serious or not? I'd love to be able to declare that some of things I have done in the past are not serious and so I do not need to go to Confession... but you have to admit I am not exactly unbiased!

And think of the words of St Paul in I Corinthians 11.27 "Whoever, therefore, eats the bread or drinks the cup of the Lord in an unworthy manner will be guilty of profaning the body and blood of the Lord."

This last statement is chilling, but then again when you actually read the words that Our Lord spoke you generally find that they have this hard edge. It is not the happy go lucky 'just do what you think is right and everything will be OK' message which some say that He brought to the world.

The stakes are high. We receive the Lord in joy when we receive Holy Communion and it is for our salvation, but it is not something that we should do unthinkingly or lightly. There is only one person in Church who has to receive Holy Communion, and that is the Priest.

Your obligation, as a Catholic is <u>not</u> to receive Holy Communion every week. It is to hear Mass. It is to be in the presence of the great Sacrifice of Almighty God. This does not mean that should never receive Holy Communion, but rather, that what the Church demands of you (for an obligation is a demand, even if it is only a demand on the conscience) is to come to Holy Mass on a Sunday, or the Saturday vigil, and to say your prayers. These prayers are joined to the prayers that the Priest offers on behalf of the Church. If we think that we have to receive Holy Communion to fulfil our obligation, then what about those who cannot receive Holy Communion?

We have to ask ourselves if it is correct to receive Holy Communion if we live contrary to Church law, if we indulge in actions which are not right, and we have no intention of changing, or even if we have just been terribly beastly to someone. If you have just had a blazing argument with your spouse and children in the car on the way to Holy Mass, and you have dragged up things that should have been put to rest, and said harmful and hateful words… then do you think that without another word being spoken between you, it is right and fitting to go and receive Holy Communion?

We need to be in a state of grace to receive the Lord, and that comes from knowing that we have been restored to that state by the might and majesty of Almighty God. How wonderful it would be if every time we received Holy Communion we asked ourselves the question beforehand "Do I need to go to Confession?" and the answer was a honest 'No'.

When there are enough priests, I love to see people going into Confession before and even during Holy Mass. You can almost see the angels pushing a sinner in and skipping with joy when they come out with their souls shining white to take their place in the presence of the saints of God around His altar.

4

I DON'T NEED TO GO TO CONFESSION

Hmmm, I wonder how many times I've heard that said. Well, actually not as often as you'd think. Usually, it is "I must go to Confession, I haven't been for ages". But sometimes you hear people say that they don't need to go. And I don't mean that they have literally just stepped out of the confessional and so don't need to go, because they have not had time to get up to anything! No this is a life defining big statement: "I don't need to go to confession."

I need to break this down into two types of people:

First there are Catholics who have been to Confession in the past and now decide that there is no need for them to go to Confession any more. And second there are non-Catholics who have theological objections to the Sacrament.

First the Catholics who have decided that they do not need to go to Confession.

The point of being a Catholic is knowing that Almighty God has put the Catholic Church on earth so that you can get to heaven. It really is that simple. Do what she says and you'll be all right. Ignore her at your peril. If you do intend to go against the teaching of the Church, then be aware that on the day when the Lord calls you from this world to Himself, and you stand before the Divine Majesty, you have to justify yourself. Forgiving a sin is nothing compared to wilfully dismissing one of the seven ways in which God had ordained that His Grace, that His Will should be carried out on earth. Namely, denying the Sacraments.

And if you have ignored the teaching of the Church, what have you said to others? Have you said that they should go? Have you said or shown by your example that it is acceptable not to go to Confession? Have you led others away from the Sacrament, so that they do not go even once a year (which means that they are in a state of grave and serious sin)? Not only have such people put themselves in a place which seems to say that they are better and more knowledgeable than the Sacrament of Salvation, the Mystical Bride, the continuation of Our Saviour Himself here on earth, i.e. the holy Catholic Church, but they have also led others in their falsehood.

I know that that sounds heavy, but just for one moment think of this.

There was a man called Frank who was so sick that his very life was threatened. So he went to the Doctor. The Doctor knew him as he had given him healing medicine in the past, but the medicine tasted bad and had some slightly antisocial side effects. The man decided that he did not need the medicine, even though the Doctor told him that his life was in danger. What is our opinion of Frank? He's a fool. If he doesn't do what the Doctor orders and becomes seriously ill, then he has only himself to blame, and if his life is seriously threatened, then we could even argue that we should intervene and force him to take the medicine.

But what if Frank, either by his example, or by what he said to others, influenced another person not to go to the Doctor and not to take medicine. Frank could have threatened their life, not directly, of course, but through his influence. He is responsible not only for his own stupid action, but also for endangering others.

This is not a laboured point, although it is a serious one. This is a direct parallel to those who ignore the need for Confession and influence others to do the same.

If a Catholic says that they do not need to go to Confession, then I ask them what have they done that they are too ashamed to go to Confession about it.

I hope that they just have fallen out of the habit of going to the Sacrament. It may be that they think that they do not need to go to Confession because they have not done anything wrong, but let me tell you that in my life I have never met a Saint! The ones who are closest too it, are the ones who know their weakness and recognise their need for Confession.

Of course some have even been told that they do not need to go to Confession anymore, that it is old fashioned and no longer necessary in this day and age. If a Priest told you that then say a prayer for him, because he has led you away from the truth, and we Priests will be judged for such things. If a priest did say that then they were wrong. Completely and utterly wrong.

If Catholics say that they do not need to go to Confession, then they have issues.

But for some who are not Catholic, then there may be theological issues that come usually from their own history. To understand this fully we have to go back all the way to the time of the formation of these groups of Christians in the heady days of the sixteenth century.

In the West the world was Catholic. The Church organised and was an indispensible part of every aspect of life. It did not intrude, it did not 'stick its nose in'. It was just there, as normal and natural as breathing. Of course there were odd practices going on in some places. This will always happen when human beings are involved in things.

In this world, there arose a group of people who did not want the power and influence of the Church in their lives. To get rid of it, they attacked the areas of life where the Church was most important, the offering of Holy Mass, and the forgiveness of sins.

It was the command of Christ Himself that Holy Mass be offered by the Priests in union with the Church. Only a Priest can do this. And it was Christ Himself who also gave power to the Priests to absolve and retain sin, for the salvation of the individual. This is an extraordinary amount of power in the hands of the Priests. And this is why the Holy Sacrifice and the absolution, the taking away of sins, has always been dealt with in the most careful and strict manner in the Church.

Getting back to the sixteenth century. Those opposing the Church wanted to attack her power, so they attacked the Priest, and they did this by destroying both Holy Mass and Confession. For them, Mass stopped being the sacrifice of God to God and became to varying degrees, a simple meal, and Confession was roundly condemned (though not, it has to be said, by the first generation of those who attacked the Church). Soon Confession fell out of practice in the 'reformed' tradition. After all, why put yourself through something that is hard and difficult if you don't have to?

This is the context that many non-Catholics are coming from. They do not understand why sins have to be, or indeed actually can be, absolved by a man, a Priest, sitting in the place of God and pronouncing the absolution, the words of forgiveness, on His behalf. For them, there is no need for anyone to stand between the sinner and God. There is no need for intercession or mediation. You see, they do not believe that God founded the priesthood expressly for this purpose and they do not believe that there is any need for anything at all, be it Church, priesthood or liturgy between the soul and God.

I will look at the question of why one must go to a priest and why we cannot just confess silently to God in the next chapter, but you can see that the statements about not having to go to Confession are very different depending on who makes them. Both of course are wrong, but the individuals are doing different thing when they say that they do not have to go to Confession.

A Catholic, if they know what they are doing, is being wilfully disobedient to the command of God, and if they do not know what they are doing then they have been misled. Either way, someone is going to have to do a lot of explaining before the throne of Divine Majesty (and remember that what is in the balance is the eternal destiny of your soul).

A non-Catholic may be closed to the truth of the faith, but he or she is not wilfully disregarding something which they know to be true, or that they should know to be true.

"I don't need to go to confession" cuts no mustard.

5

WHY A PRIEST? WHY NOT JUST CONFESS TO GOD?

This is an accusation that is often made against Confession. It goes something like: "God knows what I've done and I'm perfectly capable of telling Him that I'm sorry. I don't see why some man has to get in the way." Of course, we also have to acknowledge that it is easier to say sorry to God in the silence of your heart, rather than having to voice it in the presence of someone else, so often this question is not so much about Confession but rather the individual's unwillingness to go to the Sacrament.

As a theory it's wrong because 'a man' or rather a part of God's creation, will always be between the soul and God.

We are not angels. We do not have direct access to the divine, and we are part of God's creation. God uses this creation to communicate with us. Not only is it the way that God works, it is also the reason why the Incarnation happened. God became man, He entered into His creation, so that we could have a hope for salvation. God uses what He has made to speak and communicate with us. In Catholicism we know how God does this. It is through the Church, and the things which are contained within her, namely the Sacraments, the Scriptures, and her authoritative teaching. The classically Protestant view of the relationship between God and us denies that God designed the Church as His means of salvation. Basically, there is no need for anything between God and us, we are perfectly able to access the Divine without any help from anyone else - thank you very much. And if we do have something in between (a candle, a nice reading, something like that) then it is because we choose it. It is not necessary, and it is most definitely not something that someone tells me to do.

Except, of course, God knows better. He knows that we are not terribly good at seeing Him in His creation, or listening to His voice over the hubbub of everyday life. All too often we become fixated with the creation rather than the Creator. And when God does try to communicate with us, we twist His words so that they resemble our own and we twist His will, until it looks ever so suspiciously like what I wanted to be true in the first place.

This is why God founded the Church and gave us the Sacraments. Sacraments are the places and times when we know for sure that God acts in the world. He may be doing any number of other things, but we do not know that for sure. God gave us Sacraments so that we can be one hundred per cent sure that His grace is available for us in these sacred moments. We need someone to tell us that we have been heard and that our sins have been forgiven.

It's rather like getting the confirmatory letter or email saying that you have bought something and have paid for it. You have something physical in your hand which says that you have handed over money, or performed an action. You know that it has been done, and you can be sure of it, because this says so.

In Confession you know that your sins have been forgiven because someone tells you that they have. And not just anyone, but the person with the power, the man who God has ordained for this very purpose.

When I file my tax returns online I want to be told that it has gone off and has been done correctly. If I am speaking to someone on the telephone and I ask them who they are, and the nice lady says "I am Janet, the lady in charge of making sure your taxes are correctly paid and filled in and whatnot" then I feel I am in good hands. After all this is Janet's job. It's what she is paid for. My goodness, she went on a four day residential course in the Forest of Dean to know that my taxes are correctly filed!

But if the answer on the other end of the phone is "Barry, and I make the tea, and I'm just picking this up because Janet is on her lunch break, but I'm sure it'll all be all right" then suddenly I'm not too happy about the whole situation. Who is Barry to tell me that the forms are filled in correctly? When it comes to tea, there's no one to beat him, but not about this... this is tax, one of things you can be sure of (the other one being death). I want Janet.

You can tell your sins to your friends, your family, your therapist, your doctor, but they do not have the authority to tell you that it has been dealt with correctly. They do not have the power to assure you that the sin is forgiven. Only a Priest has that power, that authority, and he has it because God has given it to him.

It is there for your good. If you want to trust the nice lady down the road who seems to know a thing or two about being poorly instead of going to the Doctor, then good luck to you.

God has set up a system that gets rid of sin.

It's called Confession.

It works.

6

FOR OUR GOOD

Why is the Church so keen on Confession? It is not as if the Priest gets anything out of it. We sit in cold rooms for hours at a time, and then get told the tales of woe and sadness that are part of people's lives. We cannot talk about it to anyone. We cannot check to see if Confession or our advice has made the slightest bit of difference to anyone's life. We priests 'get' nothing from it.

Except… that we know that it does good. And that is enough for us, and enough for the Church. We know that it does good, not to us, but to the Church as a whole. When we go to Confession it changes us, poor sinners that we are, and we are made clean and whole again. We are members of the Body of Christ, and so when we are made clean and rejoice, the whole Church rejoices with us.

And be assured that we Priests need to go to Confession just as much as anyone else. In fact, probably more! To hear Confessions, we need to go to Confession.

The Church is our mother. She wants what is best for us. When I was growing up I had to go to the dentist. He had a beard and his fingers smelt. I didn't like it at all. He used to put me to sleep with gas, and when

I woke up my mouth was full of blood and cotton wool. I was not terrified, I just did not like it. I did not look forward to it. But to be fair, it sorted my growing teeth out.

I am not going to liken going to Confession to going to the dentist, because Confession does not evoke fear and terror. It should make us feel ashamed but that is a different thing.

Rather, our mother, the Church, knows what is best for us, and although I may not have realised it at the time, my visits to the dentist were essential. Now I skip along to the dentist with joy in my heart and a song on my lips (until they have been frozen and I can only drool for an hour or so). What my mother instructed me as a child, I now accept as a man. My earthly mother is still working on other things such as 'tidying my room', 'not leaving dirty cups around the house' etc. etc. etc., but I have to give her something to moan about!

The Church tells us to go to Confession because we should, and there are lots of selfish and stupid reasons why we will persuade ourselves that we are too big and clever to do what she says. But in the end we are only depriving ourselves of God's love. And that is just downright silly.

7

HISTORY OF CONFESSION

This is not the place for a whole scale history of this great Sacrament, and there are some good books out there. The external form of this Sacrament has not always been the same. In the early Church the practice was public confession in front of the whole community, but for obvious reasons this fell out of fashion. Your willingness to be honest changes the more people that there are around you. We can be full of bluster in front of a group and charmingly honest when alone with someone. Public confession meant that the more serious sins were not confessed. People would simply prefer to go away having said nothing rather than own up to things that they were ashamed of.

We can easily see how this could come about. In the first flush of conversion a young Christian, or Christian community, is full of ideals, and life changing thoughts. And rightly so. At this point in the conversion of a soul, there is no problem with confessing sins in public. You can tell everything about your past life… after all you have left it all behind. What does it matter what you did to who, and how you did it. That's the old you!

But when the world and the usual run of the mill things begin to tempt again, then suddenly things are very different. After all, the soul asks itself, how could I confess to that old sin? My life is supposed to have changed, and here I am falling into old sins, old habits, old vices. That was supposed to be part of my old life, not the new life I have in Christ. What will these good people think of me? How will they react to me. Better not to mention it. Or even not to go there anymore.

And this is not to mention the evil that can lie in the heart of one who takes delight in a public confession for the wrong reason, especially if it involves another person… "My dear brothers and sisters in Christ, I am a sinner! I am so nosy! I walk around at all times of the day and night, just prying into other people's business. I just can't stop myself! And so I apologise to you, Frank because I was watching the back of your house, when you crept in at three in the morning when your wife was safely tucked up in bed. And Marjorie, I looked through your windows! How terrible I am! I didn't mean to see all of that stationery which seems to come from your office at work, and I coveted it… it's so new and shiny and expensive, much more than I ever thought you'd be able to afford!" You can see what I mean.

The essential elements, of course, were there, namely the knowledge of the sin, confession of the specific sin out loud, the imposition of penance, and the words of absolution from the mouth of the Priest, but the outward form had to change. It just was not working any more.

The practice which we ended up with was more or less what we have now. All of the central parts are the same and now we just go into a booth, room or confessional and make our Confession privately, not in front of a group. When Confession became private, it became much more pertinent to the human soul. This had happened by the ninth century.

The only other thing that changed over time was the penances which were imposed. Originally these were very strict and may have involved being a penitent, weeping and sitting in sack cloth and the like for months or even years. In the thirteenth century the Irish monks who had come to Europe before had brought with them little books and charts to help Priests decide what the penance should be. Their use spread through the whole of Europe. These books, or Pentientials, were very useful, because Priests had always had the hard decision of what penance to impose. We always want to get it right. Anything that seems to help is willingly grasped.

There was a danger in the Irish Penitentials, however. They could be seen as being a little mechanical:

Spot of lying… 3 Hail Marys; being disobedient… 1 Hail Mary; taking the Lord's name in vain… 2 Our Fathers; gossiping about the neighbour… 2 Hail Marys; "So that will be 6 Hail Marys and 2 our Fathers…"

It was a bit too much like a shopping list, and the danger was that the penitent, the one going to confession, might think "let's make it up to the round 10 Hail Marys by having a spot of gluttony and lust"! Silly I know, but the focus moves from the sin committed to the cost that it had. Not good. So that practice went and the penance was restored to the discretion of the Priest.

After this slight change in practice, we have Confession as you would recognise it as it is now. Of course the form of absolution would have been in Latin. That is still possible now, and indeed in certain circumstances would be normal. There is a section on this at the end of this book. Before we could perform the Sacraments in the vernacular, they were done in the language of the Church, Latin. There is no difference, the words that take your sins away are different, that's all. The rest is in English.

So it is <u>not</u> an excuse to put off going to the Sacrament…

"I've been meaning to go to Confession for ages, but I just cannot get the grammar right. Latin is so tricky!"

8

THE FORMS OF CONFESSION

The essential parts of Confession are the statement of individual sins, the imposition and acceptance of a penance, the words of absolution and the individual performing the penance which has been set. We have seen that in the past this may have happened in slightly different ways, and so now we can look briefly at the three 'rites' (ways in which they can be carried out), which are allowed in Church. You may have come across these in your parish, though, as we will see, I hope that you never come across the third Rite!

The first Rite: Individual Confession

This is when the penitent goes to see the Priest in a confessional or in some other place which cannot be overheard. Usually, though not necessarily, it is at a regular time of the week which is advertised in the parish - "Confessions: 4-5pm Saturday evening..." But of course you can always just go along and ask a Priest to hear your Confession - "...and on request." This is the normal way that Confessions are heard. Of course, these Confessions have to be full and frank, more of which below, but they are entirely private matters.

The second Rite: Penitential Services

This second Rite of Confession is becoming increasingly popular, and like most things, it can have both a positive and a negative effect. At its heart this Rite is essentially the same as Individual Confession. We can divide this second Rite into two parts. As it is called a 'Penitential Service' we can guess that there is some form of public worship, or collective element to it. But do not fear! There is no public confession of sin!

A Penitential Service is a usually time when a number of Priests have been invited to a parish and are available to hear Confessions. The service begins with hymns or readings, and perhaps a homily. Very often there is a guided examination of conscience. This is simply a Priest reading out areas of life which you may have to think about to prepare for your Confession. It could go something like…

"As we come to prepare for this great Sacrament of God's forgiveness we think of the places and times in our life since our last Confession when we have failed to live as God has wanted us to. Have we always said our morning and evening prayers? Have we tried to come to Holy Mass on Sundays and Holy Days? Have we been attentive at Mass, or have we entertained distractions… etc."

After this, there is sometimes background music playing, or hymns sung, or the Blessed Sacrament exposed for prayer and veneration. Then you go to Confession, as in the first rite above. The penitential service takes the place of the preparation for Confession, but the meat of the Confession is same. It is individual and specific.

The good thing about the second Rite is that it means that you are more likely to go to Confession, because you can go as a family or as a group of friends. If you have the opportunity to go every week, you can easily put it off for a bit - "Oh, I have to finish this ironing, I can go to Confession next week". If the Penitential Service happens only during Advent and Lent, then you know that you have to grab this opportunity. If that is the strength of the second Rite, then it is also the weakness. Because it tends to make people think that they only need to consider going to Confession during these two seasons of the year. And of course that is not the case! And in some parishes the only time Confession is mentioned is in the context of Penitential Services.

As with many things in our faith, it should be both/and, not either/or. Confession should be advertised during a regular weekly slot as well as Penitential Services, and not just one or the other.

However, and it pains me to say this, you have to watch out when there is anything which is not a normal individual Confession. There is nothing wrong with Penitential Services at all, but sometimes Priests, hopefully for good motives, can lead people astray from what they should be doing, and tell the people things which are not right.

I have heard it said "Now, just come up and confess one sin…" - which means that there will be sins on your conscience which have not been forgiven. This is not correct. No Priest can tell you that, and no Priest is correct in telling you not to make a full proper Confession. You know what you will do… just confess to being unkind to your next door neighbour, and conveniently do not confess adultery! After all, the Priest said confess only one sin. He didn't say it had to be the worst, and what

35

happens if you have two whoppers? Are you supposed to trade your sin with the person in the queue after you? It's just wrong.

The third Rite: General Absolution

At the beginning of every Mass, the Priest pronounces the forgiveness of God over himself and the people. But this is only for venial sin. It will not get rid of serious sins, which need to be confessed in the normal way through Confession. It also does not fulfil your obligation to go to Confession once a year.

I mention this first just to stress that the beginning of Holy Mass and the Sacrament of Confession do different things.

General Absolution is very specific. It is when a Priest absolves the sins of a great number of people without hearing their Confessions individually because of a very specific set of circumstances.

The first and most obvious situation can be called the 'burning plane' scenario. It is as follows. An aircraft pilot announces that the aeroplane is on fire and everyone on it will die very soon. There is a Priest on board, who could not possibly hear the individual Confessions of everyone on board. Were he to start, he would not be able to finish before all of the penitents' sins were absolved, and some would then die in a state of sin. In this situation the Church teaches that the Priest can tell Catholics present to make a perfect act of contrition (mentally to tell God that they are completely sorry for the sin that they have committed) and the Priest can absolve the sins of all present. There is not enough time to hear all of their Confessions, so the Church allows the Priest to take away their sins in one go. There is one important rider. If the pilot is wrong and the people do not come to their end, then they have to go to Confession normally as soon as possible, and confess their sins as usual, <u>even</u> the ones they had thought about at the moment of the 'perfect act of contrition'.

A second situation is if large communities of Catholics live so far from a Priest that he can only visit once a year or even less frequently. In such a circumstance the Priest may give General Absolution, after a 'perfect act of contrition', because he will not physically be present in the community for long enough to forgive the sins of the individuals, through the normal practice of Confession. However, as above, if another Priest comes along who can stay longer, then they all have to go to Confession and confess their sins, including the ones thought of during the 'perfect act of contrition'.

The same reason may be used for a military chaplain absolving the troops (again, however, they would have to make a normal individual Confession once there is Priest available).

From these examples you can see that General Absolution comes about only when there is a real and pressing danger. Then if the situation changes, or as soon as is possible, the individuals must go to Confession as normal.

It is a sad betrayal of Confession to see 'General Absolution' mentioned in parishes in our country. Unless everyone were about to breathe their last there can be no circumstances which regularly occur under which General Absolution can be offered in this country. It is an abuse of the Sacrament. It has been specifically forbidden unless the very specific circumstances are fulfilled, and much more importantly, it does not take away the sins of the individuals.

Let me repeat that. It does not take away your sins away. If you have committed serious sins, and have been to a service where the Priest offered General Absolution, and you have not confessed those sins in a normal individual Confession since, then your sins are still on your soul.

This is not an opinion, or matter of theological style, or an old fashioned Priest like me being fierce… It is a matter of fact, and a matter of danger for your soul (not to mention the soul of the Priest who has abused the Sacrament in such a terrible way).

If this has happened, then first, make a perfect act of contrition, second, go to Confession as soon as possible, and third inform the Bishop of the Priest who has offered this so-called absolution to sort out the situation. Do not worry; you are not betraying the Priest. You are preserving him from a terrible sin. And it is the responsibility of the Bishop to do something about it.

The first two Rites of Confession are fine, hopefully you will never need the third!

9

EXAMINATION OF CONSCIENCE

So let us go through the form of Confession from beginning to end. Often it is the worry that things have changed that keeps us from doing what we know we should.

Confession begins before Confession begins… no, I have not gone mad. Confession should begin before you get to the confessional. You should set aside some time to prepare for Confession. I do not mean that you select your outfit or trim your moustache, but that you make an examination of conscience. An examination of conscience is giving yourself time and space so that you can look honestly at your life since the last time you went to Confession and see what is on your conscience. What is it that you have done that you are ashamed of, and what is it that you have done that you know is wrong?

Please note that these last two things may not necessarily be the same. We can and must confess things if we know that they are wrong even if we do not feel ashamed of them. Shame is a positive emotion which, in many cases, is a gift from God. Just because I do not 'feel' that something is wrong, does not mean that it is all right. We can deceive ourselves that the teaching of the Church is not right because we do not want it to be right. I may not feel that I should act or think in a certain way, but if the Church tells me I should, then I should.

There are good examinations of conscience in the CTS Simple Prayer Book. Buy one if you don't have one. They are just a couple of pounds. There is also an examination of conscience printed at the end of this book. No one examination of conscience is 'correct' or 'perfect'. They should just be thorough and honest.

It is funny how seldom we take time to examine our hearts and minds in everyday life. There is a great tradition in the Church of replaying the things that happened during the day just before we go to bed. This way we are very aware of the times and places that God has been present for us, as well as the needs of others, and, of course, our own failings. This mini examination of conscience means that we regularly check ourselves, our actions and motives. It makes it easier when we prepare for the Sacrament of Confession.

So, your examination of conscience has taken place and the time of Confession approaches. You have in your memory your sins to be confessed (or you have written them down on a piece of paper) and with joy in your heart you head off to Church.

How very exciting it all is!

10

THE CONFESSIONAL

Well, you have made it as far as the confessional door. You are ready, willing and able. And so here comes your first choice.

In some Churches you will be given a choice how to make your Confession. You will have the choice of making your Confession face to face, and so the priest will see you, or behind a grille, so anonymously. Please do not make it a fetish one way or the other. Sometimes you will have to make your confession looking at the priest eyeball to eyeball, and sometime you will have to be behind an impenetrable screen. This will depend on the situation or the architecture or even the opportunity.

It does not matter. What matters is that your Confession is heard. Of course, this is not a reason to be sloppy in the way the Sacrament is celebrated. But this is really in the realm of the Priest's authority. However you should always be able to have your Confession heard anonymously. Who profits if this goes through your mind...

"I am not going in that box, it's old-fashioned and I want to see the priest."

or...

"I am not going to Confession where the Priest can see my face. Confessionals were good enough for thousands of years and they are good enough now."

I'll tell you who profits... Satan. He will snatch you from Confession as soon as possible. And if you don't believe me, how long is it since you went, and what are the stupid reasons that you came up with as an excuse for not going?

Come to Confession, face to face, or behind a grille. What difference does it make? Get over it.

I prefer behind a grille, but when I need to go, I need to go...

This is the Sacrament of God's love and the only person who can stop it is you.

11

MAKING A LIST

I find that I need to write my sins down. This is not because they are so numerous that my poor brain would collapse under their weight, but rather I have a terrible memory and I want to make sure that I confess all that is on my soul.

Beware! Make sure that you destroy your list of sins after Confession, otherwise other people will be able to see what you have been up to and you will never be able to hold up your head in Morrisons again.

Just a note about it - it is sometimes difficult to remember what we had intended to say in Confession. You may not think that it is hard to keep a few things in your mind, but actually it is quite amazing how your mind can go blank when the moment comes. You want to make a good Confession, so just do anything that will make it easier. I make a list of what I want to say. I do not write it out in full, after all what would happen if it fell into the hands of an enemy? Rather I write it in note form or in little squiggles that make sense only to me...

Word of caution: do not draw pictures of your sins. Depending on what you have been up to these could be highly embarrassing when it falls out of your purse in the queue in the supermarket.

I always make sure that I destroy my list afterwards. When I used to go to Confession in Westminster Cathedral I would start shredding the thing immediately after I had finished, and continue through my penance. On the way home I would drop just a few bits in every bin I passed. I tell you, not even the best Russian spy would have been able to have put that back together again. So if you need to, then write it down and destroy it afterwards.

Also do not feel embarrassed about taking a book or leaflet into Confession to help you remember what to do. It is not a test! There are usually Confession leaflets at the back of Church. But if all else fails and so does your memory and you have no idea what you have to say or do next... then don't worry. Just say to the priest "I've completely forgotten what to do!" He will guide you through it step by step. We do not mind, we will help you in any way that we can. The 'perfect' Confession is when someone is prepared, says their sins, receives absolution and amends their life, not if they are word perfect.

12

IN THE NAME OF THE FATHER…

All of our rites begin with this basic statement of our faith. Everything finds its meaning in the action of the Most Holy Trinity. The Holy Spirit has worked in your conscience so that you know your sins and we return to God who is our Father, and we can do it because of the death of Our Lord upon the Cross. It is Jesus who forgives your sins and restores you to communion with Him. It is our destiny to be caught up in the life of the Blessed Trinity, and so we begin the Sacrament in His name.

This is the proper beginning of Confession. It is important to know when Confession begins because from this moment you are covered by the Seal of the Confessional. This means that nothing at all that you say can ever be repeated by the Priest. The seal is complete and inviolate. If, for whatever reason, a Priest were to break the seal and tell anyone what he had heard in Confession, then he is immediately excommunicated and can only be forgiven by the Pope and the relevant Vatican offices. If it were widely known that he had broken the seal, then he would never be allowed to function as a Priest again.

Nothing can be repeated, be that thinking a bad thought about someone at one end, to murder at the other. No matter what you say, the

Priest will never ever mention it to you again outside the confessional. Indeed he has to act as though he has never heard it. If you tell him that you have stolen his car and put it three streets away, he cannot go and get it, for he does not know what you have told him in the Sacrament.

Throughout our history, Priests have been persecuted and have even gone to their death for the seal of the confessional. In Northern Ireland, we faced the wrath of the police for not revealing terrorists' Confessions. In Bohemia in the 14th century St John Nepomuk was killed for refusing to reveal the secrets of the Queen to her husband. We are not protected in law for this. So if the government called to ask me if any of you had been to Confession, never mind what you said in it, I could not tell them and I would have to be held in contempt of court.

All of this, even the dire consequences which we Priests can face for the sake of the seal of the confessional, is there so that you can tell them everything that is on your conscience, be it a 'white' lie or a mortal sin.

Priests have died and will die for the seal of the confessional

13

IT HAS BEEN … SINCE MY LAST CONFESSION

The first thing that a penitent says in confession is how long it has been since the last time they went to Confession. Please bear in mind that nothing in Confession is asked or said because the Priest is being nosey, but only to inform him of what is actually being confessed.

The nature of the sin confessed could well change depending on the last time the penitent went to Confession. Also it may change the way in which the Priest deals with the penitent. IF someone has not been to Confession for thirty years, the Priest will expect a different type of Confession from someone who went last Thursday.

There is a difference between "…it has been a year since my last Confession and I have thrown the cat at my husband on two occasions…" and "… it has been a week since my last Confession and I have thrown a cat at my husband on two occasions…" Laying aside for a moment the terrible sin of cat-hurling, the first Confession says it has happened twice in a year, in the second twice in a week. As a Priest I now want to know in the second Confession how often this happens. Has this happened in the past? Is this every week? What brings it about? Is it the cat or the husband who is the object of violence?

A silly example, I know, but what if it is "I went out and looked lustfully at another woman", "I drank to excess and threatened violence", "I did not say my morning prayers". The frequency that these things happen are a flag to the confessor to see if there are other issues, spiritual or practical, that the penitent is avoiding or deliberately downplaying.

The priest does not want to know for knowing's sake, he wants to help a penitent to confess and see if there are underlying problems. The statement of how long it has been since the last Confession helps to do this. The Priest needs to know any facts that are relevant to help the individual. Remember the Priest in the confessional is a spiritual doctor in his surgery. It would be silly to go to your doctor and say "I do not care that you think that my rash is caused by a terrible life threatening disease, just give me some cream to treat this one isolated symptom".

Also if it is longer than one year since your last confession, then that in itself is a sin that has to be absolved.

14

THE STATE OF LIFE

Before we get to the confession of sins, we need to start with a statement of life. This sounds terribly bureaucratic but it isn't! It simply means telling the Priest your state of life. Are you married? Are you single? Are you a Priest? Are you in a relationship with someone?

The Priest needs to know this as it also can change the nature of the sin being confessed.

Consider the following:

"Forgive me Father for I have sinned. I went out on Saturday night and got talking to this girl. We got on very well and I took her home. I gave her a goodnight kiss and that was that."

Ah, I hear you cry, what a well mannered young man! How good it is to find someone nowadays who is so gallant, so chivalrous, such a fine upstanding member of society! Why, you could take him home to meet your grandmother. The Priest could say "My child, you have behaved as a gentlemen should. Be careful with your morality and always ask Our Lady to guide and protect you."

But what if the man had neglected to mention that he is actually married with three children,. How different the Confession is then! The state of life changes the nature of the action. No longer is it just an innocent end of a good night, but the potential betrayal of wedding vows. Indeed it could have been so much worse, but it is bad enough as it is. The sin is different. There is a victim who is not present in the confessional and indeed who was not even mentioned and that is the man's wife.

The second example is a sin.

If I, as a Priest, confess to not saying my prayers then it is worse than if a member of the laity who confesses to missing them. I have taken vows to do so, you have not. You should, I must.

Saying your state of life allows the Priest to understand what it is that you are actually confessing. And if you are behind the grille, then it is only polite! Even if I know you, I will ask during confession if you are married or not if it affects something that you have confessed. Remember that the priest does not know who you are… even if he does!

15

AND THESE ARE MY SINS

The point of Confession is, rather obviously, the confession of sins. The meat, the central element, is the work of the penitent. Confession and absolution takes away our spiritual punishment for particular sins, so for that to happen, particular sins have to be confessed.

In the past it was common for sins to be classified into 'mortal' and 'venial' sins. The difference between them was the gravity or seriousness of the sin which had been committed. We know that there is a difference between thinking a bad thought about someone and whacking them over the head with a kitchen implement! 'Mortal' and 'venial' are useful definitions, but if you like use terms such as 'serious' and 'less serious'.

This is a bit of a mine field, so here we go.

Mortal/serious sins: the big ones, the ten commandments, adultery, murder, lying to offend God, missing Mass with the deliberate intention of offending God... These must be confessed as soon as possible. Do not put them off for a week.

Venial/less serious sins: things that separate us from the love of God but do not destroy our relationship with Him. Offending others, not saying prayers, deliberately being inattentive at Mass, lustful thoughts… these do not need to be confessed immediately, but it is hard to remember them if you go to Confession only once a year.

The first lot, the mortal sins, <u>must</u> be confessed, the second, the venial ones, <u>should</u> be confessed when you are in Confession. It is important to remember that for a sin to be mortal the one doing it must know that it is mortal, know that it offends God, and still through it all, go forward with the action. That, usually, is a pretty tall order.

You have to be specific, but there is no need to involve others. The Priest does not need to know who the neighbour was whose cat you taunted, or which girl/boy is the subject of your increasingly ardent attentions (when affection turns to stalking!)

But it needs to be honest and full. It needs to be specific, because something general could cover a multitude of sins, more of which next week.

16

DO NOT TRY TO DECEIVE

We always have to remember in Confession that the purpose is to say the sin out loud and in a way that the Priest can understand.

That sounds a bit obvious, but there is the world of difference between: "I have been selfish…" meaning I did not go out of my way to be pleasant to Mrs O'Whatsit next door when I came in from night shift and was simply exhausted, but could still have stopped and said hello. And "I have been selfish…" meaning when I saw the starving children I took all of the food for myself even though I had already eaten that day, and I just know that they may not have survived because of it." It may sound the same but the sin is completely different.

Of course these are extremes and probably would not be run-of-the-mill confessions, but just for a moment think of what could be covered under the following general sins:

"I have not always told the truth…"

"I have been disobedient…"

"Sometimes I look at things that I shouldn't…"

"I sometimes gossip…"

"Sometimes I'm not patient…"

"I have judged others…"

"Sometimes I lose my temper…"

"I don't always say my prayers…"

I have done it, you've done it, we've all done it… trying to sneak one past the Priest either by mist or camouflage - mist is being so general that confessing 'gossip' covers the cruelly vindictive character assassination you carried out on the woman in the hat sitting in the third row from the front (and who you've never liked since she said your lemon drizzle cake was a 'little bit dry') - while camouflage is trying to slip in stealing vast quantities of money from the petty cash tin between nice sins: "I'm not always attentive at Mass, I do not help little old ladies across the road as often as I should, I once said someone's lemon drizzle cake was dry, I may have taken too much change from work, and I do not given enough to charity." - Camouflage!

We have to be specific. It's hard, but then so is owning up to what you have done. There are no short cuts and there is no cheap grace.

This is what I have done. It was wrong. Please forgive me.

17

HOW MANY TIMES?

So we have looked at the type of things that have to be confessed (sins) and why we have to do it to a Priest (for our good), so let us look at 'number'.

I use this term because it used to be taught that sins had to be confessed by number and type. I think that this is a useful guide, but as with all things it can be taken to an extreme which is not helpful.

Consider the following statement: "Forgive me Father for I have sinned, I argued with my wife." Well that fulfils one of the elements of confession, namely that it says what the sin is (though, of course it could be that I argue with my wife when she suggests that we spend all the money that we have for the mortgage on a series of new hats instead of giving it to the nice bank manager - in which case an argument could well be a justified result to the situation!) But what it does not say is when the last Confession was. If it was one day then I know that the incident happened yesterday, or if it was two months ago, then I know that there has been an argument in the last two months. Nor does it say how often the arguing takes place.

You see it could be a totally out of character one-off, or it could be something that happens all the time. The concern of the Priest is not just the sin itself, but also the underlying causes that could be there: just to help the penitent, the one coming to Confession, to see that there may be something greater going on, either spiritually or physically.

Does this happen often, is there a pattern, is there something that someone has to address or is it just a strange blip in character? The number of times that a sin is committed will help the priest understand what is being confessed and help him help the penitent.

On the other hand consider the statement: "Forgive me Father for I have sinned. It has been three months since my last Confession and I have sworn on 76 occasions, I have had bad thoughts about my wife's compulsive hat buying on 36 occasions and have eaten to excess 19 times." Yes, it is exact, but perhaps (and I say this only gently) perhaps a little too exact. Something in between, not one extreme or another… That's the most useful for the Priest and if it is useful for the Priest, then it is useful for the penitent.

18

WHAT I CANNOT NOW REMEMBER

We have come to Confession and made a good preparation and are through the door and are confessing our sins. This is done honestly and directly. Confession is not like having a chat with a Priest. If you want to have a chat, then have a chat, but this is Confession. He listens to your Confession and then when you have finished he asks questions or gives advice, but it is not a 'two-way' conversation from the beginning. There is a place for that in the bit that comes next, but not yet…

…for all these things and all my other sins which I cannot now remember…

You say this phrase or something like it when you have finished listing your sins. It is a bit of a catch all. You say to Almighty God "Look God, I know that there are some other things that I have done but for the life of me they slip my mind at the moment. So I'm truly sorry for them and if I could remember them then I would mention them. So if it's all right by you, we can include them as well." It's a very human provision.

Even if you have made a good examination of conscience and written down your sins, there may well be some bits and pieces that have slipped your mind. God forgives you… so don't worry. We can never remember everything that we have done, and there will always be parts of our past life that we simply don't remember. This phrase covers all of that. It is an act of humility, knowing that God's forgiveness is bigger than our sin.

However: it does not cover wilful 'forgetting'. So the 'and all other things' does not work if you decide not to mention the affair that you've been having or the cat you've been being terribly beastly too. It has to be genuine. God knows, and you know, so who do you think you are fooling?

Nor does it cover grave sins. The taunting of cats (unpleasant though that may be) would be covered if you had genuinely forgotten the incident. Adultery, because of the nature of the sin, would not. Serious sins need to be confessed as soon as you remember them. And they have to be confessed exactly.

I would say that if there is something on your mind and soul, even if it is not too serious and you did genuinely forget, then simply mention it the next time you go to Confession. It's better that way.

After all it's not as if it's going to be years before you go to Confession again!

19

LISTENING

Once you have confessed your sins, and said that there is nothing else that you can remember, you sit and listen to what the Priest has to say. Don't worry, he is not going to tell you off… necessarily!

Going to Confession is different from going to your teacher or parent or boss. They might well want to let you know who's in charge, and they may want to rub your nose in what you have done wrong 'for your own good' but generally because they can. None of this is relevant to a Priest in Confession. It may be that he might remind you of the seriousness of a sin, or the consequences of acting in a certain way, but that is all.

No, what the Priest has to say is either to elicit more information from you… "When you said that sometimes you were not as nice as you could be, what exactly did you mean?" The Priest has another agenda: are we talking about not always helping do the dishes, or stock piling nuclear weapons to unleash on your neighbour's leylandii?

Perhaps the Priest is trying to give you advice. We Priests will not (necessarily) have committed the offences that you have confessed, so we are not talking from experience. A Priest generally should not talk about his own experiences anyway, because it is your Confession not his, but we are talking from the wisdom of the Church, which we know to be correct, and from our experience of hearing many Confessions.

Advice is just that, advice. You can take it or leave it, but do listen to it. The Priest is the Doctor of the soul. And we have experience and wisdom in these matters. It may not be something that fits with your situation or which after prayer and thought you decide is something that you should or could do, but at least listen.

The Priest does not give advice for his own good, or even to see if it works out for you, but for the care and love of your soul.

20

PENANCE

After the Priest has said his bit, he imposes a penance. Sometimes people get this mixed up, usually non-Catholics who want to criticise the practice of Confession. The conversation usually goes something like this…

"Oh, that's such rubbish, you can just do what you like, say a few 'Hail Marys' and get away with it."

Needless to say that is not true. It assumes that there is a strict relationship between what you have done wrong and the penance that is imposed. Also it assumes that Confession is really just a kind of transaction.

When we speak of the relationship between sin and penance we have to get one thing straight - you do not make up for your sins by saying your penance. Penance is a sign of how sorry you are. A child breaks a Ming Vase by jumping off the sofa. He gives up his pocket money for a year. It does not even begin to cover the price, but it is a sign of how sorry he is.

The penance is a sign, for we cannot make up for the offence that our sins have caused. God loves us so much and never ever wants us to do anything that goes against what He wants us to do. When we do something wrong He doesn't stop loving us, but it does cause Him pain.

A person may do something awful and then say sorry and be forgiven, but that does not change the reality that the offence was committed. You try to make sure that it does not stand in the way of friendship and love, but you cannot undo what has happened. How are you going to make up for it? You've said sorry already... Buy a present? Replace the thing you've broken? The offence against the person is priceless. All you can do is show that you are sorry.

An argument. Words said. Hurt given and received. So what does the bunch of flowers do? Why do you now get round to doing the dishes, or doing something that you were supposed to do ages ago? What does it do? Nothing... the penance is just a sign. It is a sign that you are sorry. Just a sign. It is important, but it does not make up for the offence given and received.

Do you want to know the correct penance for the offence you gave to God by your sins?

The Cross. The Death of God. That is the acceptable penance.

And God paid for it as a sign of His love for you.

The penance is not related to the offence of the sin. The tear of God when he looks at my sins cannot be made up for through an 'Our Father' - the prayer is a sign of my sorrow.

Similarly there is no transaction between God and my sins. I cannot think "If I commit this sin, then all I have to do is say 10 Hail Marys and I'll be all right." In human terms that is the same as saying "If I kill my grandmother, then all I have to do is go to prison for 10 years or so, and I'll be alright." No, the sin scars the soul and offends God. There is no transaction.

If you give me seven pounds fifty, then I will give you a copy of my latest book. This is a transaction. The two are worth the same. I give you what something is worth and you give me the object.

In Confession there is no transaction, because we cannot give anything that is of similar value to our sins. So when someone says "All you have to do is say a prayer and then you are OK" they completely miss the point. It also cheapens the emotional and spiritual effort that you have put into making a good Confession. It is only ever said by people who do not know the liberating experience of Confession, or those who have decided that they are too holy/good/proud for the sacrament. For the rest of us, we know how hard, and yet how wonderful it is to have our sins forgiven, and to have that compared to buying a pound of bananas in the supermarket is offensive.

So, the point of this is that we know that we do not 'get off' sin by saying a few prayers. God does not hold it against us, but we will pay for our offences in the world to come, during the time of our purification in purgatory. Our sins no longer stand in the way of our relationship with God once they are forgiven, but we do have to pay the price in our small way. Purgatory does this by revealing to ourselves the implications of our actions. Only then can we hold up our heads in heaven.

What is missing from this theological way of understanding Confession is the doctrine of Purgatory. This is the place, after our death, where we make up for the sins we have forgiven on earth. The Sacrament deals with the spiritual punishment, but we have to make up for it in the afterlife. Penance on earth is a reflection of Purgatory and is something which should be embraced with joy.

22

A FIRM PURPOSE OF AMENDMENT

This is an essential part of Confession, and if you look at it one way, then it seems to make Confession impossible, while on the other it makes everything possible.

The firm purpose of amendment means that at the moment of the confession of sins, the penitent must not only be sorry for what they have done, but also must mean that they are not going to do it again. This is so simple to say, and the danger is that it can lead to the frame of mind which we have already mentioned: "You just do what you want, say a few Hail Marys and then you can do it again". This is the part of Confession which changes it from being simply an easy way to give you free license to do exactly what you want, to something you have to take seriously.

The firm purpose of amendment means that you want to change the pattern of behaviour that has led to the sin that you have committed, and that you do not want to commit the sin again. It all sounds so easy, but let's look at it for a moment. It means that you sincerely desire not to sin again. It does not mean that you will not be tempted. It does not even mean that you will not commit the sin again… but it does mean that you whole heartedly do not want to.

This can mean that what we usually assume to be the case is in fact not. So it is easier for a seasoned drinker to have a firm purpose of amendment when they wake the next morning and swear that they will never have another drink. The likelihood is that they will. But at that moment they mean what they say. They do not want to drink again. They have remorse, they see their fault and they do not want to do it again.

But what of the case of the young man who goes out on a Saturday night with the intention of getting up to what he should not. He knows that it should be confessed, and so goes to Confession, but when he makes his Confession and the Priest asks him about his actions, the penitent makes it quite clear that tonight is Saturday, and so he is going to go out again. He has no firm purpose of amendment. He has no intention of even trying to change his behaviour so that the sin may be avoided. This should worry us, because we can genuinely ask which of us really wants to turn from our sins? You see we know that we are likely to fall into the same kind of sins again, and so we can ask ourselves "what is the point of going to Confession? I never change, it's always the same."

This is the part that seems to make Confession impossible. It is just too much. A firm purpose of amendment seems too much to ask! But really it makes everything possible because the firm purpose is saying that you will try to change, you will avoid the places of sin, you will do whatever you can to turn from your old patterns of behaviour, and if you do fall again, you will walk again into the confessional and again ask for the forgiveness of Almighty God.

The firm purpose of amendment is so small, so slight, so fleeting, and so beautiful.

23

ABSOLUTION

And then the Priest raises his right hand and says:

God, the Father of mercies
through the death and resurrection of His Son
has reconciled the world to himself
and sent the Holy Spirit among us
for the forgiveness of sins.

Through the ministry of the Church
may God give you pardon and peace
and I absolve you from your sins,
in the name of the Father
and of the Son
and of the Holy Spirit.
Amen.

And your sins are forgiven.

At that moment, that very moment, when you have come from your everyday lives and have spoken your meagre sins in the confessional to the Priest, and he, in his frail humanity infused with the grace of God, mutters these few words, at that moment the angels weep tears of rejoicing and joy. The saints exult in heaven in songs of praise and heartfelt alleluias. And your guardian angel sighs in relief and love. For your soul has been reconciled to God and His grace floods your heart, mind and spirit.

The sinner has returned, and heaven rejoices. Freshness conquers where bitterness prevailed. Hope overcomes creeping despair. Shame is banished and stillness returns.

And God smiles at you, His child, with infinite love and mercy. You have come back. As He knew you would.

APPENDIX A

THE NEW RITE OF CONFESSION

<u>Preparation</u>

Spend a little time thinking about what it is you want or need to say sorry for. You can sit quietly for a few moments just to think about what you will say. You may find it helpful to write some things down so that you don't forget once you go into Confession.

Remember, the Priest will help you to make a good Confession, but remember also, how important it is to be prepared.

<u>Going to Confession</u>

Go in and see the Priest.

Begin with the sign of the Cross.

In the Name of the Father and of the Son and of the Holy Spirit. Amen.

Bless me Father for I have sinned. It has been … since my last confession.

You can then tell the Priest your sins.

When you have told the Priest what you are sorry for, then say…

For these and all my other sins that I cannot now remember I ask for forgiveness.

<u>Listen to the Priest</u>

The Priest will then talk to you about what you have said. Listen to what he has to say and try to put it into practice.

The Priest will give you a penance. This helps us to 'do something' as we say sorry to God. The Priest might ask you to say a prayer or do something when you have finished in Confession. Remember what he asks you to do!

<u>Act of Contrition</u>

You then say to God that you are sorry.

O My God, because you are so good, I am very sorry that I have sinned against you, and with the help of your grace, I will not sin again. Amen.

or:

O my God, I am heartily sorry

for having offended Thee

and I detest my sins

above every other evil

because they displease Thee, my God,

Who, in Thy infinite wisdom,

art so deserving of all my love

and I firmly resolve

with the help of Thy grace

never more to offend Thee

and to amend my life.

Amen.

Absolution

The Priest then raises up his hand and says the prayer of absolution. At this moment, through the Priest's prayer, your sins are taken away, and you are at rights again with God.

Go in peace

Try to remember to say thank you to the Priest for helping you in Confession, and remember to say a prayer for him as well. Find some time just to sit for a minute or two thanking God for His love and His goodness... and don't forget to do the penance that the Priest has asked you to do.

Confession is not something that happens just once in our lives, but a gift that Jesus gives us to help us to know His love each time we fall.

APPENDIX B

THE TRADITIONAL RITE OF CONFESSION

The penitent begins with the sign of the Cross (the Priest will say this).

In Nómine Patris et Filii et Spiritus Sancti. Amen.
(In the Name of the Father and of the Son and of the Holy Ghost. Amen.)

Then the penitent makes their Confession.

When you have told the Priest what you are sorry for, then say…

For these and all my other sins that I cannot now remember I ask for forgiveness.

Listen to the advice the Priest gives you, and answer any questions he may ask. He will then give you a penance to say after Confession

You make the Act of contrition during which the Priest says the following:

Misereátur tui omnípotens Deus, et dimíssis peccátis tuis, perdúcat te ad vitam ætérnam. Amen.
(May almighty God have mercy on you, forgive you your sins, and lead you to life everlasting. Amen.)

Then the Priest absolves you of your sins:

Indulgéntiam, absolutiónem, et remissiónem peccatórum tuórum tríbuat tibi omnípotens et miséricors Dóminus. Amen.
(The Almighty and Merciful Lord, grant you pardon, absolution and remission of your sins. Amen.)

Dóminus noster Jesus Chrístus te absólvat: et ego auctoritáte ipsíus te absólvo ab omni vínculo excommunicatiónis, (suspensiónis), et interdícti, in quantum possum, et tu índiges. Deinde ego te absólvo a peccátis tuis, in nómine Pátris, et Fílii, ✠ et Spíritus Sáncti. Amen.
(May our Lord Jesus Christ absolve you; and by His authority I absolve you from every bond of excommunication (suspension) and interdict, so far as my power allows and your needs require. [making the Sign of the Cross:] Thereupon, I absolve you from your sins in the name of the Father, and of the Son, and of the Holy Ghost. Amen.)

He may add the following prayer:

Pássio Dómini nostri Jesu Christi, mérita beátæ Maríæ Vírginis, et ómnium Sanctórum, quidquid boni féceris, et mali sustinúeris, sint tibi in remissiónem peccatórum, augméntum grátiæ, et præmium vítæ ætérnæ. Amen.
(May the Passion of Our Lord Jesus Christ, the merits of the Blessed Virgin Mary and of all the saints and also whatever good you do or evil you endure merit for you the remission of your sins, the increase of grace and the reward of everlasting life. Amen.)

Did I neglect to give a good religious example to my family?

Did I fail to take an active interest in the religious education and formation of my children?

Did I fail to educate myself on the true teachings of the Church?

Did I give scandal by what I said or did, especially to the young?

Did I cause anyone to leave the faith?

Did I cause tension and fights in my family?

Did I care for my aged and infirm relatives?

Did I give a full day's work for a full day's pay?

Did I give a fair wage to my employees?

FIFTH COMMANDMENT

"You shall not kill." (Ex 20:13)

Did I kill or physically injure anyone?

Did I have an abortion, or advise someone else to have an abortion? (One who procures an abortion is automatically excommunicated, as is anyone who is involved in an abortion. In the United Kingdom, the excommunication will be lifted in the Sacrament of Confession.)

Did I use or cause my spouse to use any medication which deliberately brought about the death of a conceived child? The morning after pill or IVF treatment, etc.?

Did I attempt suicide?

Did I take part in or approve of "mercy killing" (euthanasia)?

Did I get angry, impatient, envious, unkind, proud, revengeful, jealous, hateful toward another, lazy?

Did I give bad example by drug abuse, drinking alcohol to excess, fighting, quarrelling?

Did I abuse my children?

SIXTH COMMANDMENT

"You shall not commit adultery." (Ex 20:14)
"You shall not covet your neighbour's wife." (Ex 20:17)

Did I wilfully entertain impure thoughts or desires?

Did I use impure or suggestive words? Tell impure stories? Listen to them?

Did I deliberately look at impure things on TV, DVD, pictures or the internet? Or deliberately read impure materials?

Did I commit impure acts by myself (masturbation)?

Did I commit impure acts with someone else - fornication (premarital sex) or adultery?

Did I practice artificial birth control (by pills, condoms or any other means)?

Did I marry or advise anyone to marry outside the Church without permission?

Did I avoid the occasions of impurity?

Did I try to control my thoughts?

Did I engage in homosexual activity?

Did I respect people, or have I thought of them as objects?

Did I or my spouse have sterilization done?

Did I abuse my marriage rights?

SEVENTH & TENTH COMMANDMENTS

"You shall not steal." (Ex 20:15)

"You shall not covet your neighbour's goods." (Ex 20:17)

Did I steal, cheat, help or encourage others to steal or keep stolen goods?

Have I made restitution for stolen goods?

Did I fulfil my contracts; give or accept bribes; pay my bills; rashly gamble or speculate; deprive my family of the necessities of life?

Did I waste time at work, school or at home?

Did I envy other people's families or possessions?

Did I make material possessions the purpose of my life?

EIGHTH COMMANDMENT

"You shall not bear false witness against your neighbour." (Ex 20:16)

Did I lie?

Did I deliberately deceive others, or injure others by lies?

Did I commit perjury?

Did I gossip or reveal others' faults or sins?

Did I fail to keep secret what should be confidential?

OTHER SINS

Did I fast on Ash Wednesday and Good Friday?

Did I fail to receive Holy Communion during Eastertime?

Did I go to Holy Communion in a state of mortal sin? Without fasting (water and medicine permitted) for one hour from food and drink?

Did I make a bad confession?

Did I fail to contribute to the support of the Church?